What
Men (really) want

15 unknown strategies, for a happy relationship
to your dream man - incl. Bonus

1. Edition 04/2017

Table of Contents

Introduction

First of all i want to thank you for purchase my book. I hope i can help you understanding the male psychology, so you can understand and attract the man of your dreams easily. Well, i don't want to waste your time, so let's go!

When everyone you know is getting married or already in long-term relationships, you might feel alienated that you aren't part of this pre-marital club. You start to ponder, is there something wrong with me?

Absolutely not, some of your friends are only getting married because they are afraid of finding the perfect guy so they settle for one who works as a toilet cleaner.

We only ever accept the love we think we deserve, do we deserve someone who's like a best friend AND great in bed or someone who can count their favorite hobbies on one hand?

I'm trying to not sound too cliché but the right guy for you is out there and he's waiting for you. This eBook is designed from the perspective of a man, that way you can understand a little more about the mystery that is men.

The Male Psyche

Sometimes when we talk to guys it's similar to talking to a brick wall, there's no response and you wonder if you are going crazy. Understanding what's going on inside a guy's mind can offer an insight into their motivations and desires. This kind of data is highly advantageous when it comes to dating.

For example, men are fairly docile creatures and one way to make one smile is to encourage him to do something manly. An immediate boost to his ego can do wonders. Here are a few crazy ideas to get the point across-

• Carry a jar of pickles around and ask him to use his man strength to open it. Once the jar is opened, pretend to be amazed at his Hercules-like superiority.

• If you imitate yourself as a sports fan, a guy is going to lunge at the idea to ramble on about sports. This gives you the benefit of speeding through the dating process into the mating process.

• Hysterically laugh at everything he says, even when he announces he needs the toilet.

Anyways, this section of the book looks into how men think and things you could do about it.

Signs a Guy is Worth Dating

Before you embark on the rollercoaster that is dating, consider a few things about a guy that should ultimately determine whether he is worth pursuing or just screwing.

He's got a massive... heart

Sincerity, kindness and affection are not qualities we only ever see in the lead male character of a Disney role, real men exist with these characteristics too. A sure-fire way to observe if this reflects in a guy is to ask him about his relationship with the most important woman in his life, his mom. A healthy relationship between mom and son can affirm that he's been raised right and if you can impress his mom, you can pretty much guarantee he's going to like you too.

You can't stop touching his huge...arms

A guy that works out usually symbolizes that he is focused, determined and well-groomed. Bonus points if he has a hot body. Exercise provides tons of energy so an energetic guy can take you on romantic walks or make passionate love like a champion. If a guy has no hobbies, this should be an immediate red-flag. How does he keep himself entertained? What will you do when he's sat watching TV all day?

You don't need him but he's just so good in... making you smile

You are completely happy being single, you don't feel being in a relationship is THAT big an issue. Then he comes along. He acknowledges your independence and respects it yet you don't want him to leave just yet because he's so funny, charming and oozes chivalry. He's almost addictive and you aren't sure why. If a guy can make you feel like your first boyband crush, he might ACTUALLY be worth some but not all of your time.

He makes you feel so good on the inside and out

He should get your ambitions, hopes and dreams, put them into a blender and then make you a delicious low-carb cocktail. The right guy is deeply embedded into every aspect of your being. He wants you to be smiling all the time. He will go to great lengths to make you happy, even watching the notebook or a fifty shades of grey marathon without complaining once. He will bring out the best version of yourself even if it's been dormant for a while.

You want your friends and family to see his impeccable...personality

Although having your significant other meet your friends and family is inevitable, the time it takes to make it happen can dictate something very different. If the social gathering commences in less than a month, it is an accurate indication that something is working but if it's even sooner, then you got yourself someone to flaunt like a diamond ring.

You both want the same thing

Dating casually for the time being is fine as long as you both understand each other. Not every guy is interested in a soul mate or getting married.

What are the Differences between Mature and Immature Men?

Even though a guy might be a hot piece of ass, getting to the center of that hot ass requires some diligence. Ideally, the near-perfect guy (the perfect guy doesn't really exist, sorry) should be fairly grounded and mature.

The problem with distinguishing maturity and immaturity in a guy is figuring out whether it's just a temporary lapse or a behavioral concern that won't improve. Here's a few tell-tale signs that indicate he's too immature for you-

He never admits to being wrong

He lacks self-discipline and self-control

He can't be depended on

He only cares about things that directly affect him

He holds grudges over trivial things

If a guy has 2 or more of these qualities then you are in the danger zone. Luckily these kinds of qualities will surface early into a relationship or even during dating so you have plenty of time to abandon ship when it's sinking.

Understanding why some Men like their Distance

Men are deeply pensive creatures, they don't have the ability to express themselves emotionally as easily as women.

Not all men are confident, career-driven sex machines, some are confused about what they want in a relationship and may possibly isolate themselves to try and figure things out in their confusion. Another notable reason why men keep their distance is fear of being rejected. Guys are afraid of having their alpha male ego obliterated into tiny pieces.

Men don't want to come across as needy or clingy, don't feel undervalued if he's not showing his face around lately or if he's spending too much time in the bathroom, he could just be having a big poop.

Another plausible reason for men acting aloof with you is that guys don't want to give a girl too much attention. The main goal here is the idea that the harder and more elusive he is, the more interest is generated from the girl.

What are the Factors why men leave?

One of the best things about doing a test is usually when you are finished you receive the answers and can see where you went wrong. When men leave however, confused newly-single women are left pondering "was it something I said?" Well, maybe...

He feels like she's trying to fix him

Under their tough exterior shell lies a man battling one or two insecurities. He might be worried about going bald, finding a grey hair or just having a saggy man boobs. These are personal issues that don't need further highlighting. If you want to offer some advice or voice your concerns, do so indirectly. He's probably worrying about his imperfections but only HE can make the necessary changes. Don't get in the way of his ferocious ego. Wait for him to tell YOU why he's unhappy and listen to him conclude his own solutions. At this point, only reinforce his decisions rather than opposing his decisions. If he wants to get a hair transplant, tell him it's a fantastic idea.

He's intimidated by your success

If you have ever watched Sex and the City, there is an episode in which the main protagonist, Carrie, has a book launch whereas her partner, Burger, is still struggling as a writer. In one episode, Carrie exclaimed that some aspects of his novel were unrealistic. The relationship declined from there and Carrie was devastated that she got dumped through a post-it note. A blow to both parties self-esteem.

Being compared to other men

There is a reason why past relationships are in the past, talking about your exs to a new beau can have a detrimental effect on your current relationship. Guys want to believe that the only man you need is with you now not then. He wants to ensure he is doing everything he can right. So what if your ex-boyfriend loved to give foot rubs, your new bf can probably do something much more enjoyable like make margaritas.

Nagging

STOP! Nagging too much will eventually turn into white noise to a guy. Constant moaning, whining or just general heavy breathing when you haven't exercised can create a negative habit. This habit will eat away at your boyfriend's self-esteem and ego, cumulating into a huge argument and a passive aggressive civil war. It doesn't mean you can't tell him he's wrong, in fact, you can still do it all the time, just include a positive reinforcement too. For example:

The bad way to nag

GF: Why aren't you ready for the party? We are going to be late for the 5th time.

The good way to nag

GF: Babes, can you hurry up please? I don't want to be late. You know we can get a good spot if we arrive on time. I'll give you a hummer on the way.

Co-dependency

Men like their space and with that, they need a few days off once in a while to hang with friends. They don't want to feel pressured into staying around all the time. It's important that both of you spend time apart for social activities or hobbies. Imagine he wanted to go bench press at the gym and you decided to tag along even though you can't help in any way. He will be much happier to see you after he's had a shower and finished his workout (working out will also make him horny as hell.)

Types of Male Commitments

The underlying reason why men are disinterested in committing to a relationship varies. As problematic as it is, there is a way to pinpoint a few early warnings that a guy won't commit. To make this process easy to digest, here are a few types of men to pay attention for.

Workaholic

These kinds of guys are fixated on commitment but not in relationships. Their first love is money, anything after that is about average. Workaholic men will waste their youth chasing green paper and usually lack a personality because of it.

Jock

Athletic, strong, appeasing to the eye; these guys are easy to catch but hard to keep. Jocks are literally getting offers from other women on a daily basis and they know it. Jocks are focused on sports and anything outdoorsy so if that' not your style then move along. Jocks will spend a great deal of time working on their manufactured physique so finding time to commit won't fit into their schedule.

Horny sex fiend

This guy is constantly thinking about sex all the time. He will have a profound reputation that you will normally become aware of before even meeting him. A horny sex fiend will have a massive... libido that is difficult to keep up with. It's not that he could cheat in an affair but rather he wants to make love everywhere and anywhere. These kinds of guys are best kept at an arm's length or as a friend with benefits.

Broke-ass boy

Some men don't want to commit to a relationship because they are not financially secure. Commitment can dictate money and dating costs money. He wants to buy you things but is unable to and he will feel inferior. His biggest fear is letting you down.

Damaged goods

Men that had previously bad relationships are usually afraid about starting a new one. They worry about getting hurt again and they only way that helps them deal with it is talking about their ex. If a guy is talking about past relationships on a first date, you may find yourself feeling sorry for him but this is a clear warning sign. Keep your distance but give him time and hopefully he will figure things out.

Reasons why Men Cheat and what you can do to Stop it

When you are in a relationship, the only timing your partner should lie to you is on valentines (assuming he's about to give you a surprise). Cheating can't be justified to most people but there are two types of cheaters; cheaters who think they are doing nothing wrong and cheaters who do.

The problem of cheating is that men are far more likely to cheat than women. In movies, cheating women are always depicted as a bored housewife who has been ogling at a sexy gardener, eventually getting their rose bush taken care of. When it comes to men cheating in movies, it's almost always seen more sympathetic for the guy. The estranged wife or girlfriend is portrayed as being constantly angry and undermining their boyfriend/husband's needs.

Culture and society has progressed rapidly, women and men are much more open sexually, and women can feel empowered talking about who they have slept with instead of fear of judgmental backlash from their peers. This new sense of openness should pave the way to honesty and transparency in a relationship therefore securing intimacy. Would you rather let your boyfriend watch porn than he do it behind your back?

Although you can't always be 100% certain why or if your partner will cheat, there are a few explanations to help clarify what could be going through his mind.

He isn't brave enough to tell you that he's fallen out of love

Instead of taking some time to sit you down and talk about how he feels and where he thinks the relationship is going, he just cheats on you instead. Clearly the guy is a pussy and since you already have one, you don't need him.

He's confused about love

When a relationship starts, the beginning is intense and visceral attraction will eventually transform into longer-term honesty, attachment and intimacy. He has essentially mixed up lust and love, this can deter him from focusing on commitment.

He misses a bromance

Maintaining supportive friendships with other men is an often disregarded factor in why men cheat. His bros play an important role in his mental wellbeing and if he feels that his spouse isn't giving him space, he may lash out in unpredictable ways. His emotional and physical needs could be met by someone other than you.

He has unreasonable expectations

Patriarchy is an old-fashioned belief system that is nearly extinct but if you're newfound beau comes from a traditionally small-town family background, these particular values may be heavily instilled into him. In his mind, women must fulfill his needs 24/7 unaware of your own responsibilities. If you can't, he will feel entitled to look elsewhere. This kind of mindset is also associated with someone who is narcissistic so any signs of him bossing you around are a signal flair to fly away.

He's insecure

Sometimes being a total babe is just not enough, he feels like he's not worth your time. Whether he thinks he's too old, fat, stupid or whatever. This feeling of insecurity can manifest into ways he wants to better himself such as watching porn, being flirtatious and even cheating, in an attempt to feel worthwhile again.

He's addicted

Addiction can take many different forms such as drugs or alcohol, this in turn affects men's decision –making abilities.

Addiction can also take the form of sexual compulsivity, a way to escape uncomfortable emotions or hide from possible psychological issues, thus he might partake in sexual activity as a coping mechanism.

He isn't aware how lucky he's got it

He's in a loving and affectionate relationship. You are his yin to his yang and conversation never dries up between each other. Yet, he doesn't realize any of this. He's oblivious to living in the present and thinks he can do better when it could never get any better than this.

One of the most troubling facts being cheated on is the substantial affect it has on your mental health. Some women who have found a pattern of infidelity developed post-traumatic stress disorder (PTSD). It can also devastate your confidence and self-esteem, making dating again feel like a burden.

This emotional damage seems difficult to overcome but help can come in the form of a couple's counselor or alternatively a good group of friends who are ready to listen. Whether it's something you have experienced or possibly might in the future, remember that time heals all wounds.

Some women turn to revenge and although throwing his stuff out a window/burning his stuff/kicking him in the balls will all feel empowering, it's unfortunately a short-term solution.

Building a Foundation

Catching a guy is the easy bit, maintaining the relationship is the next challenge. In this section we look into ways to evaluate your relationship and how to improve it (assuming it's not already perfect.)

During this section, you are guaranteed to learn something new to revitalize a lost connection or even develop a greater bond with each other. Struggling relationships are not uncommon and some problems you might come across will always have counter-parted solutions.

Assessing the Relationship

Being in a relationship is the next level after dating. On this level of the game, there can be three difficulty settings; easy, hard and I give up.

There is four notable toxic behaviors between couples that can pinpoint that something is very much wrong.

Criticism

Nothing pisses a guy off more than either being blamed for something or attacking him.

Popular example: "Did you leave the bloody toilet seat up AGAIN?!?

Defensiveness

He's trying to provide you with useful feedback but you don't want to listen.

Popular example: "You look good in a black dress as well as red".

Contempt

Is there sometimes an insidious motive in how you communicate? Do you mock him or do impressions of his penis when you are drunk?

Popular example: "Listen everyone, I've been faking it for years".

Stonewalling

Do you become withdrawn from your boyfriend? Is there a lack of interaction between you both?

Popular example: "I don't want to talk right now, New York fashion week is on TV".

If any of these four behaviors are prevalent in the relationship, don't panic. Typically, every relationship will feature one of these behaviors at some point.

Developing a more empathic attitude is the start of assessing a relationship. One principle, known as COAL (Curious, Open, Accepting and loving) is frequently advised to many couples. Practicing this principle however, is easier said than done.

Assessing the relationship can be a navigational minefield, the only sure way to get to the bottom of any impending issues and ensure the relationship is what it seems and not a delusion, is to ask yourself or each other a few questions.

Ready?

Questions to ask yourself

● *Are you able to have fun together?*

Think going to see a movie or on a road trip, laughing at each other's jokes. Silently conveying to each other to do something naughty.

● *Can you share dreams together?*

Think desires, goals, and ideas. Discussing a plan for the next holiday or helping your partner practice a speech.

● *Are you able to engage in productive combat?*

Think about when you argue, is it a fight or a debate? Do you reconcile learning something new or avoid each other?

● *Can you talk about your biggest fears to each other?*

No-one should ever feel alone when they are scared, hopeless or worried. Has he got your back and you have his?

● *Can you work together on something that is important to both of you?*

Is there a power struggle in the relationship? Can you work as a team such as on crossword puzzle?

- *Can you be a loving parent to your partner?*

Life is unpredictable and your partner could one day become troubled with thoughts or suffer a terrible problem. Cherish him with love by holding him in times of need.

By going through this self-evaluation, you will develop a greater understanding about your relationship and your partner.

How to Strengthen your Bond in a Relationship

There is always going to be good times and bad in any relationship, however, different phases or situations can present a challenge which can put pressure on the relationship. Strengthening your bond is the best possible solution in the face of adversity.

So how do you create a more concrete connection? Here are a few don'ts and dos to think over.

Don't say mean things

Words that you use are powerful, if you put your partner down, you are causing serious damage. Break these volatile habits especially if you are feeling frustrated or disappointed in your partner. Derogatory comments, belittling remarks and scathing insults

Don't play the blame game

It's time to take some responsibility in parts you play when there is a problem, it's the best way to resolve problems and generate solutions.

Do let go of the desire to change your partner

You can't change someone no matter how hard you try, only themselves hold that power. When you partner feels supported and loved, he will endeavor to change.

Do focus on the specific qualities of why you love your partner

The profound moments of why this particular person makes you smile are still there, always try and remember why you love and respect him so much.

Do learn to forgive your partner

Forgiveness is the fortitude of understanding, a partner who knows that their other half is relatable and empathetic to their mistakes helps develop a deeper meaning in their relationship. Even when we feel chastised or too proud to say sorry, you know that you eventually you'll get over it. The longer you wait to forgive him for being a silly goose, the harder it is to be more relaxed and open in each other's company.

Do encourage your partner to share

When we mean share, we don't mean a piece of cake. Ask if there is anything they want to get off their minds or general concerns to get off their chest. Men find it difficult talking about their feelings but if it's a common approach, either daily or weekly, then he isn't discouraged to elaborate on personal issues that are getting him down.

Do create boundaries so you don't get upset

Everyone has limitations, doing something that you don't enjoy can cause you to feel resentful later. Your boyfriend can't read minds so discuss openly how you feel about it. It's healthy to have time apart anyways.

Don't keep secrets from your partner

Your boyfriend doesn't need to know everything about you but if you are keeping a few secrets from him, they can manifest into something worse later on down the line. Most likely, he won't even care too much. Trustworthiness and honesty is the building blocks of a successful and long relationship.

Do show appreciation in the relationship

Surprising your guy with a gift can make him feel appreciated, ensure that it is something that he would like though. Men hate photo frames or anything that suggests they need to change their appearance. Leave love notes around his place or buy him a pack of beer. Actually, he will love the beer. If he enquires why you are showering him with kindness, tell him it's to remind him how great he makes you feel.

Don't daydream alone

Tell your significant other about your dreams and hopes, ask him to do the same. Further discuss ways to make it from a dream to reality. You could learn a lot about each other in the process.

Appropriate ways to communicate your Feelings

Communication in a relationship occasionally comes to a halt, you or your partner spend time avoiding each other because you are unsure what to say about certain aspects of the relationship. How do you talk to your boyfriend? Sometimes when you talk, he's only half-listening or watching football. Here's a guideline to help open up channels of communication.

• Finding the right time

Try and find a time when you are both calm and not distracted, why not share a bath as it's perfect. If you or your partner are too busy, arrange a time and talk then. Choose a suitable location such as a coffee shop as the coffee can keep you focused.

• Don't attack him

Try to familiarize yourself with replacing negative word choices to positive ones, using negative words can make you come across as an attack. Try starting sentences with "I feel like".

• Be completely honest

The truth can hurt sometimes but it can lead into creating a healthier relationship. Admitting your imperfections and promise to stop making excuses is a step in the right direction.

• Review body language

When listening to your boyfriend, don't position yourself in a slouch, half-asleep or nodding your head profusely. Don't take a call, text or even sneeze (well maybe that's ok). Sit up, make eye-contact and face them head on.

• Utilize the 48 hour rule

If you boyfriend has pissed you off, tell him directly or you could wait 48 hours. If you are still angry or hurt after 48 hours then talk about it. If not, then just forget about it. Once you do mention that you are hurt and if he apologizes then let it go.

- **Talking face to face works best**

Don't deal with serious matters in writing, this can come across as passive-aggressive and you will feel isolated with the lack of communication. Text, letters and emails can also be misinterpreted so this could cause even more suffering on both parts.

If you makes you really angry and you want to hit him on the face with a rusty spoon, take a deep breath and remember a few points during an argument.

Take a break from the situation- Tell him you want to go for a walk or listen to some music. This should relax you otherwise maintaining an argument can escalate rapidly.

Think about the situation- What exactly was it that made you upset about and are you able to clearly explain it to him.

Listen to him- After you have told him how you feel, stop talking and listen to what he has to say. This allows both parties the opportunity to express themselves in a safe environment.

What to do when his Attention Declines

Feelings of excitement not present? Do you get more excited over the thought of eating ice-cream than eating a penis? Do you even laugh together anymore? Is there any way of knowing 100% that his attention has dwindled and he's just not seeing you like how he use to?

So many unsure questions, let's look for a practical solution or two.

Go on a date

Something to spark the memory of your first date. The place where you met for the first time. Try and reenact what you talked about and discuss how far you both have come. Bring along a few notes or questions to keep the conversation interesting.

Praise him in front of others

Your partner would definitely appreciate hearing positive feedback, especially in front of family or friends. Highlight a few perks of why he is so great. What's the one thing he does that nobody else can do?

Motivate him

Imagine you are a cheerleader and he is the football player. Chant his name every time he's doing a task, he will love it. Regardless if it's something menial like screwing in a lightbulb.

Cook for him

There's nothing quite like a good home cooked meal. Something you have really put some thought into. You could ask him to help you prepare the meal, working as a team on a cuisine can produce some hilarious outcomes.

Give him space

Let him have some fun with the boys, give him beer as an incentive. Show him how you understand that he needs some space so he can do his own thing and respect his independence. When he returns, he should be smitten to see you (especially if he's had a few drinks.)

Look like a million bucks

Looking you best can have its own rewards such as a confidence boost and feeling amazing but he will also reap the benefits. Before you know it, he's even updated his Facebook profile picture of you both even though he hasn't used Facebook in 6 months.

Make him think you need him

One of the best ways to harness his attention is by pretending that you need him. This could take the shape of help with moving heavy objects or killing a scary spider in the bath. Remember to make him feel appreciated afterwards with a hug and a kiss.

Getting the Right Guy

Where are all the men? You might ask your girlfriends this and subsequently ponder if there is a dick famine. Maintaining an interesting, fulfilling life is the most obvious agenda you should have. If you had no hobbies, interests or even friends, do you think someone would be interested in dating you? If you answered yes then you need to study some of our tips vigorously.

Define exactly what you want in a guy, if he was a celebrity, who would he resemble the most?

What kind of qualities do you look for in a guy and then make a list of places that he could potentially be located? This is an excellent start for your conquest and use a few flirtation techniques such as –

• Joke with the guy, remember to relax and don't come across as desperate or needy
• Tease him, touch his arm or his leg if you are feeling more adventurous
• Play hard to get, men will usually always initiate the kiss so you don't need to do anything until then.
• Smile, how else will he know you are enjoying the conversation?
• Swap contact details, don't add him on Facebook just yet. Tell him that he has to earn that privilege but he may follow you on twitter.

The 5 Stages to show your Interest and Secure the Right Guy

It's time to go on the hunt and get yourself a delicious super hunk of a man. The location of a man is irrelevant as you could pick up a guy even while waiting for a bus. Most men however, will congregate at a bar or club so this is worth a look. Don't go to a bar or club alone though, it could give the wrong impression and also it's safer. Getting the right guy is in 5 different stages, you already have practiced a few but just in case, let's have a look anyway.

Stage one: appearance and body language

- Don't hesitate to look the part, make yourself as sexy as possible.
- When you are in his presence, apply lip gloss so that he will pay attention to your lips.
- Play around with your hair when you talk/ Break eye contact every once in a while, this suggests you are shy around him.
- Keep your body turned towards his and turn your shoulders towards him too.
- Smile while listening to him talk, this shows you appreciate him

Stage two: flirting and the touch barrier

- Gently touch his arm or shoulder when he says anything funny.
- Make it more physical if he is teasing or give him a hug when you meet.
- Try and encourage him to touch you by saying you have strong arms/legs/butt.
- Produce a lollipop or banana and eat it while maintaining eye contact, add a wink or giggle near the end of your performance.

Stage three: compliments

- Tell him his shirt looks nice or how you has such inviting eyes.
- Get personal with the compliments by telling him he's hilarious or how it's been so long since you met somebody interesting.
- Tell him how much of a great time you are having.

Stage four: finding out his stance

- Ask him if he likes anyone or what's he looking for in a girlfriend.
- Try and make it obvious that it's your own motives rather than sounding like a friend.
- Tell him you are open to having a boyfriend casually.
- Discuss qualities you like in a guy or list things that make a guy special.

Stage five: Securing a date

- Casually talk about upcoming plans and mention your schedule.
- Wait for him to ask if you want company.
- Use some common interests to your advantage such as seeing band or an event.
- Tell him about an interesting bar he should visit and invite him.

So there you have it, it's really that simple. You should go from single to mingle in no time.

How do you Know he wants to Commit

A woman's worst nightmare can come in the form of a guy who's a commitment-phobe. Time is usually the most reliable test in knowing for sure however there are a few things to look out for when deciding if he's ready to commit.

Intention

Think about the word choice used by a guy, is he using "hang out" or "date"? Date suggests a bit of commitment. If he asks you to want to hang out, get him to elaborate if he means a date?

Consistence and reliability

Is he pre-planning with you a few days in advance or only to meet tonight? Does he expect you to reschedule? Is he always on time? If he is interested in commitment, he will value time spent with you and that you are a priority to him.

Direct communication

After a date or two, a guy who wants a relationship calls or messages you again after a few hours or even after a few days. If it's been two weeks, he's not ready to be serious.

Exclusiveness

Is time spent with you based on being alone together or rather with a group of people in a social gathering setting? He should want to get time allocated to knowing more about you instead of you being a convenience.

Talking about a relationship

After a couple of dates, it's time to bring up the question. Keep it light-hearted and simple. One method is talking about his goals and asking where you are with him.

Things you Shouldn't say to a Guy

You know when you are blatantly rude, mean or crazy with a guy can have a negative impact. These actions can cause a guy to shut down, impacting a strain in the relationship. To prevent triggering any harmful reaction is a few sentences to remove from your vocabulary.

"You are so much better than the other guys I've date."

This says a lot more about you than him, comparing him to your exs looks bad, extremely bad.

"Are you able to afford that?"

When it comes to finances, men don't want to hear how to spend their money. Negative remarks such as this mean you will start to feel more isolated and left in the dark.

"We are running late. Don't worry."

Reminding a guy that he is running late isn't going to help the situation, this dissenting nagging leads to him eventually not listening to you.

"I haven't done that in so long, don't be ridiculous."

Just because you are now in a relationship doesn't define that you aren't any fun anymore. Have an open mind and consider a different perspective.

"Is your hairline receding?"

Never ever talk about a guy's hair or insinuate that he is going bald, ever.

He might blush off your comments but deep down there's a feeling of resentment. He may even interject and talk about your weight or how you shouldn't leave the house without make-up.

"How many people have you slept with?"

Way too personal, never good ever comes with asking this kind of question. It implies you are assuming he is some kind of secretive Casanova or is hiding something from you. A real blow to the trust in the relationship.

"You are getting too big?"

Remember that you can't change a guy and that only he can do so with himself. Suggesting he has gained a few pounds is hurtful to his ego. Why not instead subtly declare that you want to join a couple's fitness class or go for walk because it's a nice day.

Avoid Getting Played

Tired of investing time into a guy only to find out he was a waste of space? How can you protect yourself from getting played? Generally players are easily spotted in a club or even on social media, they usually have a gym picture uploaded every 2minutes.

Solution: openness + boundaries = Success

Here's a few things to consider when dating or meeting someone-

Guys with low self-esteem

A guy with low self-esteem is much more likely to be a player. Why? He needs constant validation that he is good enough for girls. A confident guy shines bright like a beacon in the night so aim to gravitate towards him.

Family values

The relationship the guy has with his family can indicate a few things. If he is apprehensive about talking family then this could be a red flag that is has difficulty with relationships.

Bad behavior

Things such as ignoring what you say or disappearing randomly shouldn't be tolerated. This guy's bad habits are obvious and he's not worth your time.

Actions speak louder than words

Sometimes what a guy does is an indication of his personality rather than what he says. Is he making time for you? Does he keep his promises? If no, then get rid of him.

Wait to have sex

If the guy you are dating is genuinely interested, he won't mind waiting to have sex with you. This shows he respects your boundaries and doesn't want to intrude or upset you.

Conclusion

To conclude this entire book, I want you to know that it is possible for you to understand the mind of the typical man. For you to do so, you must follow all the information and advice that this book consists with. As I told you before in this book, with hard work and patience you'll surely find the perfect guy to hold a committed and everlasting relationship with.

Also, if you enjoyed reading this book or find that this book holds some sort of value, then it will be very much appreciated if you could leave a positive review on this book. I want to reach as many people who wish to find love in their life through this book and by you leaving a positive review, it will surely help me accomplish that. You might even get some massive good karma!

And once again, thank you very much and the best wishes to you and your journey.

Here are some other books of mine, which may can be interesting for you ;-) Make sure, you check it out!

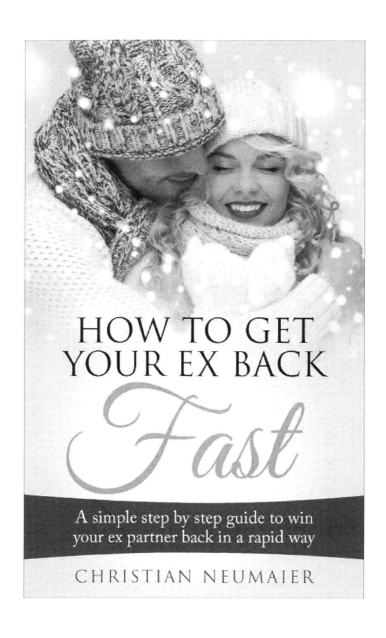

HOW TO GET YOUR EX BACK *Fast*

A simple step by step guide to win your ex partner back in a rapid way

CHRISTIAN NEUMAIER

How to win the HEART OF Your DREAM MAN

16 Unknown, proven strategies to attract the man of your dreams

CHRISTIAN NEUMAIER

Legal notice

Christian Neumaier

Heini-Dittmarstr. 12a

86159 Augsburg

Germany

Email: cn-lifestyle@gmx.de

VAT identification number: **DE 303277043**

Taxe: 103/254/70041

     103/254/70076

Images and graphics used:

https://pixabay.com/

Cover created by https://www.fiverr.com/creativelog

https://www.shutterstock.com/de/image-photo/handsome-elegant-business-man-looking-camera-258706064